IMAGES OF ENGLAND

Around Nailsworth
& Minchinhampton
From the Conway Collection

Building houses in Park Road, 1922.

IMAGES OF ENGLAND

Around Nailsworth & Minchinhampton
From the Conway Collection

Howard Beard

NONSUCH

Children in a meadow across the valley from Watledge, *c.* 1910.

Opposite: The 1911 Pageant of Progress.

First published 1994
This new pocket edition 2005
Images unchanged from first edition

Nonsuch Publishing Limited
The Mill, Brimscombe Port,
Stroud, Gloucestershire, GL5 2QG
www.nonsuch-publishing.com

British Library Cataloguing in Publication Data.
A catalogue record for this book is available from the British Library.

ISBN 1-84588-189-3

Typesetting and origination by Nonsuch Publishing Limited
Printed in Great Britain by Oaklands Book Services Limited

Contents

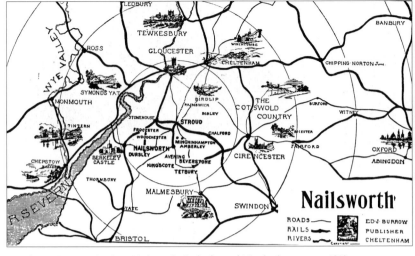

Map from a Burrows Guide to Nailsworth, Amberley and Minchinhampton, *c.* 1910.

Acknowledgements

Collecting, comparing and arranging Conway's photographs was pure pleasure. However, without the willing help of a host of friends and acquaintances, several now deceased, the preparation of this book would have been immeasurably harder.

I am especially indebted to Ann Makemson, Nailsworth Town Archivist, for all her interest, patience and enthusiasm; also to Wilfred Merrett and Ken Parker for generously making their own photographic material available to me.

Invaluable background information was supplied by Stanley Gardiner, Nick Hurst, Betty and George Mills, Frank Simmonds, Cyril Turk and Ronald Woodward.

I am also grateful to:

F. Adams, J. Allway, Miss H. Benjamin, B. and C. Bruton, D. Burton, R. Close, D. Cope, D. Flagg, Mrs. V. Harvey, Mrs. V. Holborow, Mrs. P. Ind, E. Inwood, Mrs. M. Jenner, C. Muller, M. Nicholls, Miss H. Pegg, Miss P. Pinnell, Mrs J. Porter, D. Saunders, P. Sawyer, V. Shellard, J. Simmonds, Mrs. C. Stevens, Mrs. K. Tavinner, Mrs. P. Webb, B. Wilkins, Miss M. E. Woodward and M. Wright.

Finally, my grateful thanks to my wife, Sylvia, for her constant help, advice and encouragement.

Outside 'Locksley', Conway's house in the Bath Road.

Introduction

The purpose of this book is to celebrate the work of the Gloucestershire photographer E.P. Conway.

As automation accelerates the tempo of change in the twenty-first century, the slow-moving tranquillity of Conway's England – secure, self-sufficient and unaware of impending upheaval – holds an increasing fascination for the student of social history. The small country towns of Nailsworth and Minchinhampton, together with a handful of nearby villages, were Conway's chosen territory. Here he recorded uncluttered streets, long-vanished shops, sleepy landscapes, horse transport, local festivities and, above all, village people – especially children, whose aprons, caps and toys bring so many of his photographs to life. Conway was not unique; many rural and industrial areas were served by equally gifted men. One thinks, for instance, of Murray Dowding of Chipping Sodbury, Chapman of Blockley or, nearer to home, W.F. Lee and Mark Merrett of Stroud. But, within his small locality, Conway is important because he, more than any other photographer, was responsible for recording its Edwardian pictorial history.

Eustace Price Conway was not of local origin. He was born on Boxing Day 1874 in Abergavenny on the Welsh Borders. His father, John Harris Conway, was a coal merchant. From the maiden name of his mother, Lucy Mary, Eustace acquired his middle name, Price. He had a sister Annette. There may well have been other siblings, but they do not appear to have accompanied him to Nailsworth, as did his sister and mother.

Established around 1905, Conway's business was run from a house called Locksley at the junction of the Bath and Bristol Roads. He is known also to have worked from a wooden studio in the garden of a house nearby, number 4 Victoria Villas, and, perhaps at a different period, from a similar building in Kettle Alley.

Around 1927 Conway left Nailsworth and settled in Mitcheldean, first at York House, then later at Townsend House where he died on 5 March 1946 at the age of seventy-one. His Will, made in 1934, is a somewhat uninformative document in which he gave his sister a life interest in his estate. After her death it was to be divided between the surviving children of his uncle, Octavius Price.

Advertisement from a Burrows Guide, c. 1910.

E.P.Conway was remembered by several of the older residents of Nailsworth as a slightly curious figure with a limp. One described him as 'a spidery little man in dark clothing.' He apparently travelled around with his photographic equipment over his shoulder. His trade advertisements make it clear that he considered himself an artist as well as a photographer and, together with his sister, who appears to have been somewhat flamboyant, he gave lessons in drawing, painting, marquetry and crystoleum – whatever that may have been! At a time when subdued colours were fashionable, Annette was remembered as wearing red stockings. She always carried an umbrella, whatever the weather. Conway's only transport was a bicycle, so it is not surprising that the area he photographed extended no more than two or three miles from Nailsworth.

Some, but not all, of Conway's photographs carry serial numbers. The earliest one datable by an associated event is number 700, the 1907 Minchinhampton Baptist Sunday School Treat. By 1911 he had reached 2500; number 6064 is the 1919 Peace Carnival.

Conway's postcards often bear a simple rubber stamp on the reverse reading 'Conway, Nailsworth' or, less frequently, a more decorative stamp in Gothic lettering: 'E. and A. Conway, Nailsworth.' Without such a stamp, however, his postcards are still easily identifiable since his curious handwriting of captions comprises mainly lower case letters, but with a capital A throughout. He also writes a distinctive g, y and f and occasionally, though inconsistently, a Greek e, as these examples show.

Few examples of Conway's vast portrait output have been included here; costume detail apart,

they are of little interest to the local historian. The pictures chosen comprise around one third of all Conway's topographical photographs known to the author. For the purpose of grouping them meaningfully, three sections seem appropriate: firstly Nailsworth, secondly Minchinhampton and, thirdly, the other villages. Carnival photographs generally appear at the end of each section. Occasionally, in order to achieve a particular sequence, parish boundaries have been ignored. For instance, included in the Minchinhampton section are not only Box and Longfords, which rightly belong there, but also Burleigh, Hyde and The Highlands, which do not.

Conway's work, both in technique and composition, shows indisputable expertise. All his pictures are real photographs rather than printed images and his focusing is generally tight, enabling significant details to be successfully enlarged. More important, however, is the insight his photographs afford into the social fabric of rural communities a century ago. In this regard their value as pictorial history cannot be overestimated.

One

Nailsworth

Nailsworth from the 'W', c. 1910.

Nailsworth from Rockness. Until a century ago Nailsworth enjoyed neither civil nor religious parish status. Like its larger neighbour, Stroud, it developed as a result of a natural process of population growth at the meeting point of several valleys. This process accelerated considerably during the second half of the nineteenth century and was recognized by 1900 in the rebuilding of the church. Out of portions of Horsley, Avening and Minchinhampton parishes the new civil and religious parish of Nailsworth was created. Conway photographed the town from several vantage points. This view, showing most of Nailsworth's newer buildings, highlights Gig Mill Pond and, beyond it, Johnson's Mill Pond, which served as the town swimming pool and which we shall see in more detail on page 22 and 23.

Nailsworth from the Shortwood Road. The Baptist Chapel, now Christ Church, is to the left, with Chestnut Hill House immediately behind it. In front of the chapel is Tremayne's corn-milling business.

Nailsworth Hill. During the early years of the century, stone was still being extracted close to the lowest bend of the 'W'. Note the quarry spill clearly visible in the picture.

The Park. The sweep of Park Road, still uninterrupted by development, can be seen in the above photograph of around 1910. Tanner's Piece, the parkland enclosed by the road, was used both for recreational purposes and, occasionally, as a market. The two views on the right, together with one on page 2, date from 1922 and show the construction of the houses along the northern portion of the road. The building firms employed were E.W. Baldwin of Nailsworth and J. Simmonds of Minchinhampton. Stone brought from Rowden Quarry via the old coach road through Hazel Wood was crushed on site, using a paraffin engine, then mixed with cement. The resulting reconstituted blocks formed the main external building material for this project, which was overseen by the Nailsworth Housing Company. Coal ash went into making blocks for interior walls.

The Cross in 1870. Here Conway has reissued a much earlier picture, possibly by one of Nailsworth's Victorian photographers, Alfred de Rozier or Paul Smith. In the road, the man with the bowler hat is reputed to be a Mr. Wright. Standing outside the ironmonger's shop on the left, slightly behind the lady, is the proprietor, Samuel Newman, co-founder of Newman Hender and Co. Ltd.

Looking up to the Cross from Fountain Street. In this late Edwardian view the Wilts and Dorset Bank building between Bath Road and Market Street has replaced the one in the previous photograph. Later, the site was cleared for a second time. The shop fronts on the left have also changed considerably.

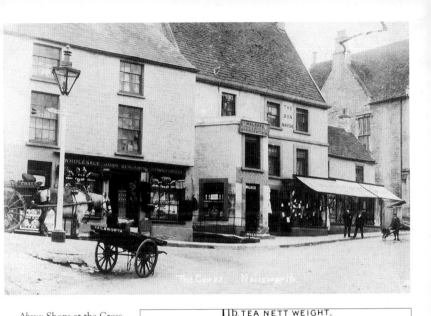

Above: Shops at the Cross. The building on the left is John Benjamin's grocery store, with Henry Evans' coal-delivery wagon parked at the kerb in front. In the foreground stands Harold Fletcher's fish cart.

Right: John Benjamin, Grocer. As this advertisement shows, John Benjamin's business was already some seventy-years-old when the above photograph was taken.

1 lb. TEA NETT WEIGHT.

WHOLESALE & FAMILY GROCER,
CORN, FLOUR & PROVISION MERCHANT.

ESTD 1841. (3RD GENERATION.)

John Benjamin

THE CROSS,
NAILSWORTH.

The Cross from the Churchyard. The tight focus and clarity of this splendid photograph of The Cross make it technically one of Conway's best pictures. The enlargement of the central portion (below) shows an advertisement board publicising the Historical Pageant of 1911, thereby fixing precisely the date of the photograph. Various scenes in the Pageant featured different historical periods: Nailsworth contributed tableaux of the corn and bread riots of the early Victorian era. (See pages 58 and 59)

Road works in Market Street. Sewerage pipes were laid in Market Street in 1909. Here we catch a glimpse of the lower part of the street leading towards Cossack Square. In the second picture the photographer faces Edward Benjamin's grocery business, run by another branch of the same family which owned the stores at The Cross.

Market Street. Though unsigned, this photograph has been included because, on stylistic grounds, it would appear to be Conway's work. In any event it is a superb view of the main stretch of Market Street. A gap now exists in the row of shops on the left, giving access to a car park approached from Old Market. The enlargement below provides a charming study of Edwardian children's costume.

MARKET STREET, NAILSWORTH.

June 11 1923

Wm A Davis

Dr. to **OSBORNE SAUNDERS,**

Plumber, Gas & Hot-Water Fitter,

PAINTER and DECORATOR,
STOVE and RANGE FITTER.

Water Supplies, Cisterns, Water Closets, Baths, Lavatories, and every description of Plumbers' Work fixed in the best manner.

SANITARY WORK CARRIED OUT WITH ALL THE LATEST IMPROVEMENTS.

ESTIMATES GIVEN FOR ALL KINDS OF REPAIRS.

To Painting outside of Cijdartha
as per estimate £ 17 10.

The Island in Cossack Square. These buildings on the island in the centre of Cossack Square, including Saunders' plumbing business, were demolished in the 1950s. The advertisement is an interesting one, with its gaslighting fitment and vintage plumbing accessories. On the right of the photograph can be seen a corner of Allway's Hygienic Steam Bakery whose flour loft and stabling were on the island behind Saunders' premises. The road through to Old Market was later opened up alongside the bakery.

Butcher Hill's Lane. Perhaps the most commonly photographed corner of old Nailsworth, Butcher Hill's Lane (as it should be correctly called, rather than Butcher's Lane) joins Market Street to the Bristol Road. The three dormers have now gone.

Cossack Square. Across the road from Stokescroft, perhaps the finest period house in the town, stand two workmen. It is believed they were excavating a gas main. In the early sixties Stokescroft was used as accommodation for retired ladies. It is now a solicitor's office. The woman in the dark skirt is Mary Bruton.

Brewery Lane. Note the unusual windows of the cottage on the left. A sweep is to be seen on the right of the group. During the 1931 floods, residents had to escape from these buildings through upper floor windows.

Bath Road. This picture shows Victorian development in the Bath Road, just below Conway's house. The condition of road surfaces in the period before the general use of tarmac is obvious.

Bristol Road from the Swimming Pool. Johnson's Millpond, lying between the Bristol and Old Horsley Roads, served for many years as the town swimming pool. The enlargement below shows the Nailsworth Swimming Club's hut, the diving board and one of the water-polo nets.

The Swimming Pool. Here a group of bathers can be seen in the cordoned-off learners' area of the pond. The water at this point would appear to be some three to four feet deep.

Bristol Road. In this photograph of the descent to Mill Bottom, with Ernest Brinkworth's carpentry, joinery and undertaker's premises on the right, the relatively treeless state of Rockness is apparent.

Harley Wood. This is an attractive hamlet and has changed little. Note the derelict buildings bottom right.

Horsley Road. These cottages stand a little further along the Horsley Road. A century on, children would be ill-advised to pose in the middle of such a busy thoroughfare.

The Fisheries. Midland Fisheries were founded at Malvern in 1882. The firm had not been in Nailsworth long when Conway produced this postcard, which is postmarked 1913. The land must have been only recently flooded since trees stand in one of the ponds.

Newmarket. The George Inn is seen here, now newly re-opened, is seen here in the days before traffic along the approach to this area became a problem. The publican in 1908, when this view was probably taken, was Henry Nicholls.

Hillier's Factory, Newmarket. Isaac Hillier was born in 1797, son of a local pig killer. A man of great business skill, from a humble stall in Market Street he developed an extensive bacon-curing concern business which came to dominate the Newmarket valley. By the time of his death at the age of eighty-eight, Hillier owned considerable property and had built himself Newmarket Court, known locally as 'The Mansion'. His industrial premises were known as 'The Trade'. This photograph, taken around 1920, shows three delivery vehicles at the factory. On the left is 'Colonel' Porter and, in the white coat, Frank Pinnell. Sadly, the firm has now closed down and the site has been redeveloped.

Hillier's Factory. This picture of the inside of the factory was taken on the landing where the smoked bacon was stored. We see, left to right, John Maller, Toby Farmiloe, Hubert Niblett, Kate Bick, Miss Abbott, Harry Clark, Albert Turk, Cyril (Tom) Turk and Frank Pinnell. The attractive advertisement below appeared in the 1901 *Gloucester and District Directory*.

Above: The Nodes. Further up the Newmarket valley stood The Nodes Mill. It was demolished in the early 1920s. Highwood Cottages, right, became derelict much more recently. The fine period house on the left, also called The Nodes, still stands today. It was built, by extending existing cottages, for Isaac Hillier's son, Peter.

Below: Newmarket. Highwood Cottages appear again in this picture. In common with many photographers of the period, Conway realized that by including local children in his foregrounds he increased his sales potential.

Newmarket. This somewhat similar view, taken a little further down the valley, has Nodes Mill cart shed on the left. The children provide a particularly fine costume study, as the enlargement below shows. Note the carved stone lion and human face which still survive. The hoist on the building beyond has gone. The reverse of the postcard says that the girl marked with a cross is Amy. Who Amy was is uncertain.

Watledge. In Kelly's *Gloucestershire Directory* of 1910, George Woodward's joinery and undertaking business is listed at Watledge. The young man in the dark clothes, leaning against the fence on the left, is in fact the fourth generation of Georges, the first being born in 1798. This George was born in 1890. His brother, Leslie, eight years younger, is standing on the path near him. The cart loaded with timber is owned by the building firm of E.W. Baldwin.

Opposite above: Miss Woodward's School. Lilian Woodward, aunt of George, ran a small school in Watledge, at one period attended by the author's mother. This photograph was taken around 1916. Standing, far left, is Marjorie Allway. Front row, third left, is George Poole, with Ronald Davies half hidden behind Ken Guy far right.

Opposite below: Watledge. This cottage, Glendower, a little further along Watledge, was later the home of the poet W.H. Davies, whose best-known lines are probably:

> 'What is this life if, full of care,
> We have no time to stand and stare?'

A plaque on the wall now commemorates him.

"Glendower"

Fircroft, Watledge Hill. This house was almost new in 1908 when the photograph was taken. Note the man on the ladder, painting the weatherboards. At one time George Wedel, who played cricket for Gloucestershire, lived here.

Shortwood. As with so many early photographs, this view is interesting because it highlights the extent of subsequent building development. It dates from around 1914.

The Pines, Shortwood. This house, with its tidy garden and modest croquet lawn, can be seen slightly right of centre in the preceding photograph.

Shortwood Village. The charm of this scene lies in the washing hung out on lines and bushes in the garden of the cottage in the foreground, now called Little Hollow. It is postmarked 1909.

Shortwood Green. Children pose appealingly in this late Edwardian postcard. The message reads, 'This is just come. I ordered it last week. Hold it to the window and you will see the pinhole through our door.' (Now marked with an arrow.)

Forest Green. In this well-balanced picture, The Jovial Foresters' Inn is on the extreme left. The large double-gabled house, together with the smaller roadside cottage near it, have been replaced by a car park. The Star, on the right, still stands, but is now a private house.

Forest Green. This distant view is taken from the opposite side of the valley, at the top of Snake Lane by Dunkirk Manor. Housing development has drastically altered the hillside. The Congregational Upper Chapel, long demolished, can be seen top left.

Forest Green. The Lower Chapel, also Congregational, was demolished much more recently in the early 1970s. Around 1920 W.H. Davies lived in a house called The Croft, on the left of the chapel.

Forest Green, Distant View. The animal in the foreground belonged to the family of
C.W. Jones, the Nailsworth coal merchant. It was kept as a pet, rather than to assist with
coal deliveries. Note Conway's whimsical caption!

Dunkirk Mill. This industrial complex, which contained at various times a cloth mill,
hosiery factory and walking-stick business, has now been partially converted into flats.
The pitched roof of the rectangular building in the foreground was destroyed by fire, then
replaced with a flat one. Its pitch has now been restored.

Inchbrook church Sunday School treat, 1907. A portion of a larger photograph is included here because of its excellent period costume. Note the girl with callipers and crutches, also the boy emerging from the hedge in the background.

Inchbrook church. Built in 1865, Inchbrook's iron church has now been demolished. Its portable font is today in St. George's church, Nailsworth.

Devil's Elbow.
Nailsworth. 708

Above: Wood Lane. Here Conway has photographed the sunken trackway leading up the hill from the playing fields in Nailsworth. Still gated and now a bridleway only, Wood Lane was once a coach road. E.W. Baldwin's carts used it to bring down stone to be crushed into building blocks for the houses in Park Road.

Left: The Devil's Elbow. Largely unchanged today, this woodland scene is reminiscent of the work of P.L. Smith, Nailsworth's photographer of the 1890s, who took many such views.

Opposite above: Chestnut Hill House Rred Cross Hospital. The Clissold family, who founded Nailsworth Brewery, had lived here for some fifty years when this picture was taken. During the First World War the house became a V.A.D. hospital.

Opposite below: Hospital interior. Here a soldier's wounded leg is dressed. Note the medical equipment on the trolley and what appears to be a primitive breathing tube hanging in the corner.

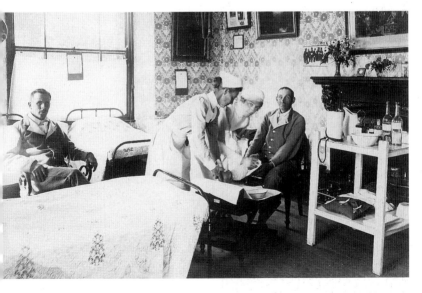

The staff and first six patients. Mrs. Wilson, described as the Commandant Officer, is seated. Miss Skrine, Quartermaster, is slightly to the right behind her. 'Our six first patients,' the postcard proudly proclaims. They arrived on March 20 1915 and mostly stayed about a month. Their names are Cpl. W.H.Smith, Pte. H.Lambert, Pte. H.Mellor, Pte. T.Walton, L.- Cpl. A.H.Hinsley and L.- Cpl. M.Corr, though which is which is unclear. The hospital visitors' book has survived and in it Rfmn. Bushell, 4th King's Rifles, wounded near Ypres, wrote the following couplets: 'We are but little soldiers meek, We earn but seven bob a week. The more we work, the more we may: It makes no difference to our pay.'

Opposite above: Fountain Street. Dated around 1913, this fine postcard shows the Post Office, with its truck for transporting mail from the station. Next door is Jeffery's cycle and motor works, with a good display of advertising plaques. Around 1930 the fountain, which gave the street its name, was moved to Old Market, only to be moved again later to its present position.

Opposite below: Dauncey's Tailors and Outfitters business. Beyond the fountain in the above view are Dauncey's shops. Next door to each other and owned by members of the same family, one was a tailor's business, the other an outfitter's.

1 & 2, Bridge Street, Nailsworth, *May 29 1903*

Mr *Benjamin*

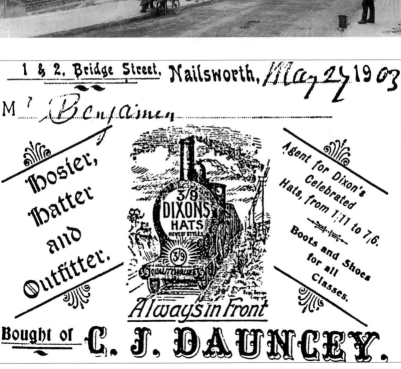

Hosier,
Hatter
and
Outfitter.

3/9
DIXONS
HATS
NEWEST STYLES
3/9
EQUAL TO ANY 6/6

Always in Front

Agent for Dixon's
Celebrated
Hats, from 1/11 to 7/6.

Boots and Shoes
for all
Classes.

Bought of C. J. DAUNCEY.

Nailsworth Post Office. A splendid group photograph, this was taken around 1910. Second left is George Woodward, fourth left Harry Mynett. Ernest Belcher is second right; Mr. Soulsby, seated and hatless, is the Postmaster.

Co-operative Society premises. At this period, the Nailsworth branch of the Cainscross and Ebley Co-operative Society was in the Bath Road. Now demolished, it was used during the Second World War as a Civic Restaurant. The manager, Mr. Arthur Park, is standing on the left.

Co-operative Society Golden Jubilee celebrations, 1913. An inter-branch competition was held as part of the festivities. The Nailsworth shop window display won second prize. The enlargement below shows not only the range of products sold, but also the skill of its window-dresser.

Spring Hill, the Upper House. This creeper-clad house has considerable charm. The two ladies potter around the garden with their dog. The gardener appears to have tactfully left his wheelbarrow and withdrawn from the scene while the picture is taken.

Barn Close. The building on the right was formerly a farmhouse, the part on the left farm buildings. The name Penowl no longer survives.

The Hollies, Nailsworth Hill. The central portion of this house, which enjoys a fine view over the town, was built in 1823. The west wing was added in 1875. The well-stocked greenhouse, with its potted palm, no doubt also dates from the latter period.

The Steppes, Cossack Square. Once known as 'Cyfartha' this double-gabled house is now a retirement home.

Bannut Tree House. This building, incorporating portions of a medieval chapel, was run for many years as a school by Miss Ellen Tabram, whose family had owned it for much of the nineteenth century. Bannut is an archaic name for a walnut.

Nailsworth Bowling Green. Situated on high ground behind The George Hotel, this green must have provided a superb setting for a leisurely game on a warm summer's afternoon.

Nailsworth Station. The Nailsworth branch of the Midland Railway was opened from Stonehouse in 1867. Later, via Dudbridge, another short stretch of the line linked Nailsworth with Stroud. In this photograph the cattle pens can be seen, with the station itself beyond. Far left is the water tower.

Nailsworth Station. An Edwardian view of the platform itself shows no less than eight members of the station staff. Among the advertisement plaques visible are those for Mazawattee tea, Camp coffee, Phoenix Fire Insurance, Bryant and May's matches, Oliver's boots and shoes and Duck Son and Pinker's pianos.

The Railway Hotel. A coal cart and Davis' horse brake are parked in front of the hotel, which sells Bowly's beers. Chamberlain's mill chimney can be seen on the right. High Beeches is top left with C.W. Jones' coal business in the foreground. The firm's offices are across the yard. The nearer building is daytime stabling; delivery horses were stabled overnight in Minchinhampton.

Station Road. This picture, with the station buildings in the background, was taken around 1906.

Traction Engine at Work. This important photograph of a contract engine at work around 1910 was taken in the angle formed by the Bath and Bristol Roads. The man with the stick is Ralph Benjamin, who owned Ringfield Farm.

Above: Club interior. One of a pair, the location of this fine photograph is uncertain, but the religious picture on the far wall and the jugs of water on the table suggest it may have been a temperance club.

Below: H.J.H. Kings' Factory the Lot Mill, Newmarket. During World War One this engineering business went over to munitions production. The men on the right, wearing caps, are Arthur Sawyer and, in front of him, Bert Wilkins. Miss Aldridge is front left with Ben Cambridge the foreman behind her. In the centre, in white, is Miss Freeman.

Missionary Exhibition, 1921. This pair of photographs of children dressed in oriental costume records an event apparently staged by St. George's church, since Revd W.F.Wood, vicar from 1915–1922, is the clergyman on the left in the Indian tableau, with Sheila Warren far left. Mrs. Gosling stands in a corresponding position in the Chinese picture.

Miss Agnes Newman's Bible Class, Newmarket House, 1919. A pillar of the Shortwood Baptist community, Miss Newman retained the loyalty of her students, many of whom stayed with her all her life. Back row, left to right: Fred Payne, B.Sawyer, V.Creed, P.Hyde, Percy Wilmott, W.Tocknell, D.Bevan, ? King, Albert Porter. Front row: George Davis, Revd F.T. Smythe, Miss Newman, Harry Bullock.

Opposite above: Feeding the ducks at Johnson's Mill Pond. The reverse of this postcard says, 'Mr Ernest King's grandchild mixes the morning mash. Ducks are at their best when reared – as these – beside a mill dam.'

Opposite below: Potato Digging at Pensile House. This photograph was taken in the summer of 1915. On the right is Gladys Dauncey, daughter of William Dauncey, tailor, of Bridge Street, whose premises we saw earlier. Her sister Kate is in the centre. Note the black armbands suggesting a family bereavement.

Feeding the hens. In this postcard Randolph Bruton, whose family still run a hardware business in the town, is seen in a garden off Newmarket Road. The card was sent in December 1910 to an address in Canada.

The Ladder, Nailsworth Hill. Motorcycles were frequently tried out on this most testing of gradients. The one shown here is a Bradbury 3 wQ H.P., dating from around the start of the First World War.

Ringfield Farm. In this splendid photograph of working farm horses, with Mr. Holborow on the right, Ralph Benjamin is wearing the light-coloured coat.

The Curate, St George's church. Revd Geoffrey Simms-Reeve was curate at Nailsworth from 1923 to 1928, when he was appointed to a parish of his own near Rugby. His machine is a Triumph Model 4 3 Qw H.P., made around 1914.

Coronation Day, 1911. This view, taken outside the church, shows the men who were responsible for putting up the street decorations. The postcard is captioned, 'Hoisting Flag.' The site was later used for the town war memorial. Front left, with the bowler, is Lemuel Price; Randolph Bruton, wearing a trilby, stands right of the lamp-post; seated is Joe Smith and third right front is Samuel Dauncey.

Portraits. Conway's portrait work was extensive. Such photographs are clearly of limited public interest and, for that reason, have not often been used in this book. These two, however, give just a flavour of his style. The first is of an unknown lady in Dutch national costume. The second shows a young cyclist, clearly proud of his machine, in Park Road, near its junction with Bath Road. Conway's house is on the left.

Dance group. This charming picture is of children from Nailsworth school. The girl on the front left is Rosie Leonard.

Chamberlain's Factory Football Team. The picture here is of the players in their 1913–1914 season. In the back row are, from left to right, -?-, -?-, P.Yarnold, S.Cowley, W.Robinson, Bill Hooper, A.Dyer, Mr. Chamberlain, -?-, George Brown. Middle row: ? Brown, George Arthurs, Roy Harrison. Front row: S.Harrison, Percy Rudge, -?-, Percy Grant, Paper Beale (so called because his reply to questions always began, 'On paper...').

The Pageant of 1911: Corn and Machinery rioters. The Mid-Gloucestershire Historical Pageant of Progress, to give it its full title, was written by Frank Gwynne Evans. It was a kind of verse celebration of the more significant episodes in English history affecting this area. The Pageant was staged at Fromehall Park, Stroud, on the 2nd, 7th and 9th September of that year. John Jacob was responsible for the music, Miss Seymour Keay for the costume and the Pageant artist was Maxwell Armfield. Different episodes in history were allocated to various towns and villages around the district. For example, Amberley, Avening, Minchinhampton and Woodchester's contribution was entitled, 'Godwyn and Gytha, around AD1050.' Nailsworth portrayed the riots of the 1840s. In this splendid photograph the corn and machinery rioters are seen assembled in a field at Watledge, before setting out by train for Fromehall Park. The author's mother, *née* Vera Lee, who died in 1993 at the age of ninety, is the little girl of nine kneeling up in the front row.

Opposite above: Bread rioters. Here we see the companion photograph to that opposite: the bread rioters. It is unclear where it is taken, but it is thought to be outside the wooden hut that was Conway's studio and which several local elderly residents said they recalled.

Opposite below: Nailsworth Carnival, 1911. This is the first of a series of carnival photographs from Conway's camera. Preceded by a police escort, a band makes its way up Fountain Street. The newly built Masonic Hall is in the background.

Bread rioters, Paignton

Above: Nailsworth Carnival, 1911. In a field below Ringfield Farm, the decorated bicycle competition entries are marshalled.

Below: Nailsworth Carnival, 1912. Another year, another procession, but Conway is still at his favourite vantage point on the bank by the church. This time we see competitors for the fancy-dress parade.

Co-operative Society Carnival Float, 1913. Outside W.H.Smith's shop at The Cross stands the Cainscross and Ebley Co-operative Society's carnival entry in their Golden Jubilee year. The small boy on the balcony has a grandstand view of the procession. Following a break during the First World War, carnivals took place annually until 1931. After that nothing happened on a regular basis, though various events, with sheep dog trials and dog racing, took place intermittently during the next few years. The enlargement is a close-up of the decorated float itself. One can only assume that the cartons and packets were stuck or pinned in some way to the substructure of the display.

Nailsworth Carnival, 1914. The carnival this year is said to have taken place on the very day in August when World War One was declared. Here fancy-dress entrants wait, presumably for judging, in the field below Ringfield Farm.

Peace Carnival, 1919. The winning float from the first post-war carnival is pictured at the bottom of Tetbury Lane. The building in the background has been demolished. Ralph Benjamin, in a Union Jack waistcoat, holds the reins.

Peace Carnival, 1919. This photograph may show either the preparations for, or the clearing up after, the carnival. The banner over the street reads, 'All honour to our fallen heroes.'

Peace Carnival, 1919. This picture shows some of the Peace Carnival fancy-dress competitors photographed in Park Road. George Cole, third left, appears as Charlie Chaplin, which he apparently did on several occasions. Second right, in the top hat, is Charlie Hooper; Harry Williams is third right. Note the small boys – Dilly and Dally!

Nailsworth Carnival, 1921. Taken ten years on, almost to the day, this picture makes an interesting contrast to the 1911 Carnival photograph. The band is in a similar spot, as is the photographer, but gone are the boaters and large floral hats. The musicians may be the Nailsworth Town Band, newly founded in 1919.

Nailsworth Carnival, 1923. The girl on the left, Marjorie Jenner, *née* Allway, was fifteen when this photograph was taken. She was dressed as a marguerite.

Portraits. Here we see a somewhat younger Marjorie, this time in December 1909, at the age of eighteen months. In the second portrait Dorothy Marshall appears, in an undated carnival picture, dressed as Britannia. She worked in W.H.Smith's shop and lived all her life in the same house in the Bristol Road.

Nailsworth Carnival, 1923. Bruton's float passes up Fountain Street. The white horse is Gertie. Bought at Gloucester market, she proved somewhat shy of traffic, but always pulled the firm's carnival entry.

"Boy Blue"
1919.

"The Mad Hatter".

Fancy-dress competitors. The last of this series of Nailsworth Carnival pictures is a delightful study, taken in 1919, of George (left) and Leslie Pool, as Boy Blue and The Mad Hatter respectively. George lived later at Cobden Villa, Walkley Wood. Leslie, sadly, died at the age of fifteen.

Two

Minchinhampton

Minchinhampton, from Forwood.

Chirstmas Card Multiview, c. 1908. Minchinhampton offers an interesting contrast to
Nailsworth. An important market town and wool centre from medieval times, its ancient
boundaries also included the modern parishes of Amberley and Brimscombe, together with
Watledge and other parts of present-day Nailsworth. Minchinhampton, almost totally built of
local stone with tiles to match, has little of the red brick and Welsh slate which bear witness to
Nailsworth's nineteenth-century development. The Parish Church of The Holy Trinity retains
early work in its south transept, together with memorial brasses. The tomb of an Astronomer
Royal, Dr James Bradley, is in the graveyard. Many quaint architectural features make
Minchinhampton an interesting town to explore, while its solid Market House still regularly
serves the purpose for which it was built. However, the town's most appealing asset is surely the
magnificent Common which borders it, attracting many visitors, particularly on warm Sunday
afternoons during the summer months. The photograph above is one of the composites in
which Conway specialized. Here he has taken eight postcards of the town, laid festive greenery
around them and created a Christmas card.

Opposite above: Holy Trinity church. This photograph was taken to mark the dedication, on 13
June 1909, of the new lych-gate built by the firm of Harman in memory of Mr. Edward Playne.
Note either side of the gate the new stone which has not yet weathered and softened to match
the older material surrounding it.

Opposite below: Minchinhampton church from the South-West. The garden on the far side of
Bell Lane, from which this photograph was taken, is now in two parts, as the house it served has
been divided. The two properties are known today as Church House and Bell Lane House.

Minchinhampton church from the market square. Here we see a superbly composed picture of the top of the High Street with the Parish Church's medieval south window in the background. The bay window has gone from what is now The Crown Inn. Note the gas lamp with its head removed. It was the task of the building firm of J. Simmonds and Sons to take off the lamp heads, clean them, store them for the summer and replace them in the autumn. They also arranged for workmen to light them at dusk during the winter and turn them off at 11 p.m. In this photograph the children are especially delightful: the one on the right has a toy train.

Minchinhampton churchyard. A Sunday School parade enters the west door of Holy Trinity church. The modern porch room is now built on to this part of the building.

Minchinhampton church. The interior of the church is little changed, except that the chancel and nave are today separated by a rood screen which his family gave in memory of Harold Woollcombe-Boyce of Windmill Road, who died on active service in 1917. Also, the chancel now has a finely decorated ceiling and the walls are rendered and painted white.

Minchinhampton.

The Market Place. This is arguably one of Conway's finest pictures of Minchinhampton. Note The Ram Inn on the left, once known as The Pen & Hand. The seventeenth-century Market House is a particularly fine example of its kind and dates from the reign of William III. Erected by Philip Sheppard, it is the sole survivor of the three the town is said to have had: one for meat, one for corn and one for wool. The Market House was given to the town almost a century ago by Major Ricardo. Sarah Siddons is reputed to have acted in it. On the right is the back of Lower Island.

Opposite above: Friday Street. A family pose at their door around 1907. Note the summer gas lamp on the right.

Opposite below: Lower Island. The buildings here, sometimes called The Old Institute, were demolished shortly after the First World War and the war memorial was built in their place. At various times Lower Island housed a rifle range and was used for school cookery lessons!

73

The Cross, *c.* 1905. This view is taken from West End, looking over The Cross into Tetbury Street. The building on the left is Viner's drug store and livery and bait stables. In the right foreground is Gabb's butcher's premises and, beyond it, Ogden's drapery store.

Tetbury Street. On the left is The Baptist Institute which, at this period, around 1910, was a temperance boarding house. Beyond it is the chapel with which it was connected.

The Cross. This view taken from the High Street shows Ogden's and Gabb's. Note the draper's well-filled window display and the pony and cart outside the butcher's shop.

Ogden's. This advertisement is taken from one of the 'Borough' pocket guides, published by Edward J.Burrow of Cheltenham around 1905.

The High Street. Casseldine's barber's pole is prominent on the left of this clear, well-focused Edwardian picture. The right side of the street has been considerably altered by the insertion of a bay window in what is now The Kitchen. The road does not appear to have been recently swept.

Well Hill. This postcard dates from around 1907. The ladies on the right are standing outside a small shop which features in the next two pictures. The Royal Oak is in the far distance down the hill.

Right: Miss Jones' Shop, Well Hill. Emily Jones is in the doorway of her fancy drapery store. The window display on the right suggests that she also sold stationery and postcards. Her assistant, Miss Wall, later became Mrs Alcock.

Below: Shop interior. In this atmospheric view of the inside of a typical Edwardian shop, now a private house, Miss Jones is on the right and Miss Wall in the centre. The name of the girl on the left is unknown.

Lower Tetbury Street. Conway took this photograph from outside the Post Office. The building set back on the right is Joe Price's forge. He stands in front with his assistants, near the platform used for putting metal rims on cartwheels. Several rims may be seen leaning against the wall of his premises.

The Coffin House, King Street. Rich in social history, this photograph is important for its costume. Note especially the lady and child on the right. The house may have acquired its name from its unusual shape, or from the undertaker who occupied it during the nineteenth century.

Above: Park Terrace. Windmill Road can be seen on the right, before widening took place; Cuckoo Row is to the left. Park Terrace, far right, was built in 1833 for Gatcombe estate workers. The story goes that one day, while driving past, Colonel Ricardo, Lord of the Manor, objected to seeing washing hanging out at the front of this terrace. In consequence he gave the tenants the land at the back so that laundry would stay discreetly hidden from view! He is reputed to have sold the whole row around 1900 for £1,000.

Right: Park Terrace. Joe Hatherall and his two sisters stand outside a house in Park Terrace around 1905. Note the bootscraper set into the wall and the neat front garden.

West End. This fine photograph looks down West End towards The Cross. Note, on the wall, the winter gas lamp complete with glass frame and mantle. The enlargement of part of the picture illustrates the costume of local children in Edwardian times.

West End. In this contrasting view looking the opposite way, the children are not the same, being generally younger. A small donkey carriage approaches.

Windmill Road, c. 1908. Many of the houses in Windmill Road were built in the first years of the twentieth century: in fact the one behind the telegraph pole is still under construction. The stone used in the semi-detached properties on the right came from the demolition of Forwood Brewery.

Forwood. This hamlet has changed relatively little over the years. The large pedimented building on the left is Forwood Grange.

Ball's Green. This postcard must date from around 1915 though, curiously, it was not posted until 1935, long after Conway had left Nailsworth.

Ball's Green. The buildings shown here are the same as in the last photograph: the shaped yew tree is common to both. This view is taken from the lane leading down to Longfords Mill.

Tetbury Road. Hollybush House stands in the angle formed by Tetbury Road and the lane to Crackstone.

Minchinhampton Common. Mothers, babies and children relax in the sunshine on the Iron Age bulwarks near Tom Long's Post.

The Comon. The house on the right is called Christowe. It was the home of the Woollcombe-Boyce family. Its wooden stables, which must then have been quite new, still survive. The half-timbered buildings on the left have been totally replaced by a stone-built property called Everest.

The Common. These houses border the Common and overlook the Chalford valley. The one on the left is now called Tom Long's Cottage. The middle one, Boscobel, has been extensively altered and the next, Park Bungalow, is now largely obscured by trees. Park House is on the right.

Park House. Mainly hidden by foliage and climbing shrubs, Park House was occupied by Mr. Robert Brodie when this photograph was taken around 1910.

The Park. In Conway's day, as now, animals grazed the Common as they had for centuries.

The Rectory. Now much extended, this building, later known as Stuart House, functioned until recently as a social, educational and recreational centre for the disabled. Around 1920 Anglican Sunday School Treats were held here, with swings set up from the trees in the drive.

Gatcombe Park. This finely proportioned house was built at the end of the eighteenth century by the Sheppard family and passed to the Ricardos in 1814. It is currently the home of The Princess Royal.

The Lammas. The story of this elegant property begins in the reign of Edward I, when it was held by one Peter de la Mere and apparently known as Lamers. It was occupied successively by the Pinfolds and Cockins, before being bought in 1876 by the Baynes family, who lived there when this photograph was taken.

Highliffe. This pleasing residence is in Butt Street. Before the houses on the far side of the street were built it enjoyed good views of the Park.

The Sycamores. Now called Reddings, this large house has been significantly altered. In 1909, when the photograph was taken, it belonged to Colonel Sir Thomas Lemmon, who had bought it three years earlier.

Box Green. Surely one of Conway's best photographs, this view of Box Green illustrates how a group of people can bring a picture to life. Probably taken in 1914, the photograph is thought to show Mrs Norton with her children Kitty, on her right, Grace, on her left and baby Joe in the pushchair. (See enlargement.)

Box Village. The Beehive Inn has long since stopped selling beer. Around 1920 the landlord was a Mr Mortimer, who also ran a butcher's shop from the annexe adjoining the public house. On the left can be seen the iron Mission Chapel, now replaced by Box church.

Burleigh. The top part of Brimscombe Hill is seen in this picture, taken from Jacob's Knoll.

Burleigh. This view looks down the hill towards Wall's Quarry and Brimscombe. The building by the roadside at the first bend, now a private house, was formerly The Bell Inn.

The Highlands. John Griffiths Frith built this large half-timbered house overlooking Nailsworth. It was completed in 1873. Since 1918 it has been the home of Beaudesert Park, a Preparatory School named after the village in Warwickshire from which it moved. Until 1995, the school was run by descendants of its founder. The current Headmaster is J.P.R Womersley. This view is of the northern side of the building.

The Highlands. This picture of the lower, southern side of The Highlands was taken at the time of a fête or garden party in 1907. The enlargement shows a band playing on the terrace, while visitors stroll among the formal flower beds.

Hyde. In this rural scene, with Ivy Cottage in the foreground, hens and ducks wander about freely.

Hyde Court. At this time the home of Henry Blenkane Beale, Hyde Court is an interesting example of a building which is basically a conventional four-gabled Cotswold house, but which underwent architectural additions at various periods.

Hyde Lodge. In this winter picture note the boy on the grass, restraining his dog from approaching the photographer.

Hyde Chapel. The Victoria Memorial Mission Hall, in the eastern part of Hyde, was dedicated in 1902. The cottages beyond have not altered significantly.

The Round Tree, Hyde. Where 'The Round Tree' was it has not been possible to discover. If it was as ancient then as it would appear to be from this photograph, certainly nothing will remain today.

Longfords House. The Longfords estate and mill were bought in the mid-eighteenth century by the Playne family, who later built themselves this fine residence. Note how well the carefully planted gardens were maintained.

"Longfords" from Avening Rd
GBA

Longfords Lake. In 1806 the great lake was completed and, in its original form before silting took place, was fifteen acres in extent. Amusingly, Conway found it necessary to paint onto this excellent photograph a large, somewhat clumsily-drawn swan!

Sunday School Treat, Longfords, 1921. In this appealing photograph of the visit of the Sunday School children from St. George's Church in Nailsworth, Charlie Brinkworth is seated among the upturned instruments. The two boys in the centre are, left to right, Bill Dean and Frank Adams. Mr Park is far left. Miss Mortimer appears, right, with her class. To the right of her are Walter Furley and his brother. Fred Vick is between the two boys and Miss Mortimer.

Longfords Show, 1913. The lady in this photograph seems somewhat unimpressed by the produce display! The show was principally for exhibiting flowers and vegetables, though there were also games for the children. Glass jars with candles inside hung from the trees to create atmosphere in the late evening.

Baptist church Procession. The final part of the Minchinhampton section of this book is devoted to Church processions in the town. In Edwardian days Sunday School Treats took place around Whitsun, the Anglicans on the Monday, the Baptists the following day. When Anglican Treats ended in the 1920s the Baptists took over the Monday. This picture shows an Edwardian Baptist procession outside the chapel in Tetbury Street.

Holy Trinity Procession. The Anglican procession of 1912 passes up Bell Lane.

Baptist church Procession. This, perhaps the finest of all the Sunday School Treat photographs which have survived, shows the 1907 Baptist procession in the High Street. The reverse of this postcard is quaint. Whether the message is intentionally amusing is not clear.

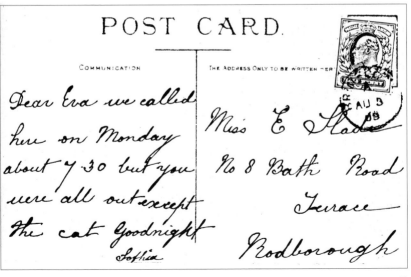

POST CARD.

COMMUNICATION

THE ADDRESS ONLY TO BE WRITTEN HERE

Dear Eva we called here on Monday about 7.30 but you were all out except the cat Goodnight
Softia

Miss E Slade
No 8 Bath Road
Terrace
Rodborough

Baptist Church Procession. The route of the Baptist procession of 1908 was along West End, where it performed a U-turn around the band before heading back into town. Wagons later took participants to a farm on the way to Cirencester, where games and refreshments were provided. A detail from this photograph shows a close-up of the musicians.

Three

The Villages

Amberley, Avening, Horsley, Kingscote, Rodborough and Woodchester mark the extent of
Conway's territory, though he made occasional forays into Ebley, Cashes Green, Randwick
and other places.

The Amberley Inn and Victoria Memorial, from the common.

Scenes From John Halifax, Gentleman. In 1856 Mrs Craik (Maria Murlock) wrote *John Halifax, Gentleman*, while staying at Rose Cottage, Amberley (bottom right). This composite postcard features other Amberley views, The Bear at Rodborough, Dunkirk Mill at Inchbrook and scenes in Tewkesbury, all of which appear in the novel.

Enderley Flat, Amberley. Enderley was the name Mrs Craik gave to Amberley in her book. Leaving a baby in its pushchair in the road at this point would not be recommended today!

Amberley Ridge. A short walk from The Bear Inn is the spot where Conway stood to take this photograph. The view, however, has changed dramatically, since today both the hillside in the foreground and Amberley Ridge on the horizon are almost totally obscured by mature trees.

AMBERLEY RIDGE PRIVATE HOTEL.

Telephone:
2Y Amberley.
Postal Address :
**Amberley
Ridge,
Rodborough,
Nr. Stroud.**
Gates open on
Minchinhampton
Golf Links.
Beautiful Views
from all
Windows.
Situate 700 feet
above the sea
level.
**Lounge,
Billiards,
Croquet,
Tennis.**

*R. A.
Thompson.*

Amberley Ridge Hotel. This advertisement is taken from an Edwardian guide to the area.

Amberley Church. Holy Trinity church was opened in 1836. Full parish status was gained for Amberley in 1840. The first incumbent, Revd R.E.Blackwell, photographed most of his parishioners in the 1860s, which has resulted in a unique pictorial record of village personalities at this early period.

Amberley School. Children were educated in the rooms beneath the church prior to 1887, when the present school was opened. Note the two little girls dressed in their Sunday best.

General view of the centre of Amberley. Photographed from a grassy rise on the lower side of Culver Hill, this picture takes in most of the centre of the village from The Lamb Inn on the left to Epworth Terrace on the right.

Spriggs Well, Amberley. This attractive view shows the road from Pinfarthings, looking towards the church which is just visible in the distance.

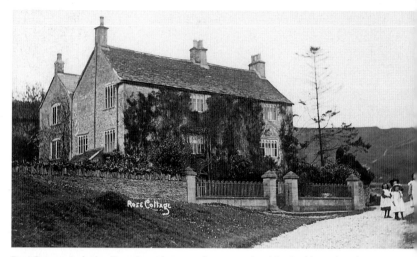

Rose Cottage, Amberley. Since the mid-nineteenth century, when Mrs Craik's novel made it famous, Rose Cottage has been firmly on the tourist map. Note the attractive Gothic windows.

Littleworth Methodist Chapel, Amberley. As the central wall plaque records, this Wesleyan Chapel was built in 1790 and renovated in 1887. It flourished during the nineteenth century, both its congregation and Sunday School totalling well over one hundred and fifty members.

The Laurels, Amberley. This stone built cottage, right, with Lower Littleworth House behind, now has a conservatory and, on the far end, an extension put up around 1953. In the distance, far left, can be seen The Bunch of Nuts.

Grayling House and Yew Tree Cottage, Amberley. Grayling House, near the war memorial, has changed little. Today Yew Tree Cottage, on the right, has two dormer windows. Beyond the wall in the distance now stand the buildings of Marling Close. The animals add considerable charm to this picture, taken around 1906.

Cottages near Amberley War Memorial. These cottages have not changed a great deal, though the one on the right has lost its slate roof and both are without their ivy. It is amusing to note that Conway tried unsuccessfully to erase from his negative a telegraph pole and its supporting cable in the foreground!

Pinfarthings, Amberley. Pinfarthings Cottage, shown here, is one of the most attractive period homes in a hamlet which has more than its fair share of such buildings. It was once two dwellings.

Avening church. The interior of the church remains substantially unaltered today, though the altar rails, choir pews and reading desks were replaced soon after this Easter photograph was taken around 1906.

Avening church. The church stands on rising ground near the school and the stream. It contains much important Norman work, especially the north door and some pillar capitals.

Nag's Head. Photographs of this attractive, isolated hamlet are rare. It takes its name from the inn standing at the crossroads left of centre in the picture.

Above: Delivery man, Horsley Road. This photograph, one of Conway's finest, might equally well have appeared in the earlier Nailsworth section. How Nathaniel Dyer, cake-vendor, would have coped with modern health regulations is uncertain, but here he sits contentedly on a wall at Swan Bank, no doubt on his way to make deliveries in Downend and Horsley. Where Nathaniel lived is not known, but his daughter later kept a shop at Washpool.

Right: Nathaniel Dyer. This second photograph of Mr Dyer is not confirmed as Conway's but, one feels, has to be included since it is so obviously a partner for the first. It is the only other known view of this delightful character at work.

Downend. The road from Nailsworth to Horsley touches the lower side of this pleasant hamlet. At one time a tunnel existed below the road, giving access from the houses on the right to the main nucleus of Downend on the left.

Horsley, distant view. This picture, taken near Barton End on the Bath Road, shows the village of Horsley across the valley. The road to it from Nailsworth passes the houses on the extreme right. The Priory is the large square building on the left in the middle distance.

Hartley Bridge, Horsley. This small group of cottages lies near the stream on the road between Horsley and Tiltups End. The unobscured building shown in the picture now has an extension.

Horsley. Through the village runs the Nailsworth to Wotton-under-Edge road. The cottages on the hill leading up from Nailsworth have altered: the wall on the right has gone and demolition has resulted in a gap below the gabled house.

Horsley. This picture looks down the main road. The school is on the right. The house on the left has gone and the one beyond it is substantially altered.

Horsley. These buildings appear in the distance in the photograph above. The Boot Inn, facing left, has given way to a car park. The large bay window on the left has also gone. Charles Franklin's grocery store is on the right. This picture dates from around 1909.

Horsley. The Bell and Castle, left, still serves as the village pub, though the large bell over the inn sign has disappeared and the chimney has also gone. The building has been considerably extended at the front.

Mount Pleasant, Horsley. The main road runs between the hedge and this terrace, which lies on the upper side of the village. The largest of the four cottages now has its central upstairs window blocked.

Horsley church. St. Martin's church remains unaltered today. The photograph dates from around 1906.

Horsley Vicarage. Now called Blackberry Hill, Horsley Vicarage stands on a wooded hillside above the road from Nailsworth, between Rockness and Downend. This picture was taken from across the valley, near the Bath Road. The incumbent at the time was Revd C.H. Badcock.

The Priory, Horsley. The building is now bereft of its creeper. The Priory was recently, for a while, a nursing home.

Horsley Post Office. This picture is of the old Post Office when it stood at the top of the narrow lane leading down to Washpool. The photograph is a delight. The cottages still survive today, though the bay window and shutters have gone and the Post Office front door is now blocked.

Washpool. As its name suggests, this is the hamlet where the little valley stream ran through a stone-lined pool in which sheep were dipped. Grooves can still be seen where boards were inserted to raise the water level and fill the pool.

Washpool. This second picture of sheep-washing is equally attractive. The cottage on the left has recently undergone extensive restoration.

Washpool. Here Washpool is seen from high land on the Barton End side of the valley. Several buildings shown on this photograph have disappeared.

Horsley, Empire Day. Empire Day, May 23rd – chosen because it was Queen Victoria's birthday – was still at this time widely celebrated with flags and patriotic songs. Here a band plays as a Union Jack is paraded.

Horsley. These cottages are in the main street, almost opposite the school. The one on the left, now called Old School House, is considerably altered, while the one behind the telegraph pole remains much the same. The two properties on the right have disappeared and the site now belongs to Hand's Garage.

The Pinnell family. Emmanuel and Rose Pinnell, right, lived in a cottage on the upper side of Horsley, where it is believed both this and the next picture were taken. Their son, Charles, is beside them with his wife Rose junior and baby Ivy. On the left is Albion Gawthorpe. All the others are Emmanuel and Rose's children: (left to right) Carrie – who married Albion – then Frank, George, Walter and Nell.

The Pinnell family on their smallholding. The pigs in this delightful farming scene are believed to be Gloucester Old Spot, now a rare breed.

Above: Kingscote church. The church of St. John the Baptist is a medieval building in the Early English style. It is hard to imagine, in this view of 1908, how the creeper could possibly have encroached any further over the masonry.

Left: Kingscote Windmill. The mill, which stood a short distance off the road to Nailsworth a couple of hundred yards out of the village, was already a ruin at the turn of the century. This indistinct view, taken from a composite postcard of Kingscote, is probably its only surviving pictorial record and is therefore of considerable importance.

Opposite above: Kingscote Park. The Georgian mansion in this photograph was the home of the Kingscote family who had lived in the parish since the twelfth century. The house was demolished in 1951.

Opposite below: Kingscote Park. Its spacious orangery was obviously well-stocked and maintained when this picture was taken around 1907.

Kingscote Park
779.

Kingscote Park
478.

Kingscote Woods. In this pleasing study of light and shade, note – in the enlargement
– initials and the date 1893 carved on the tree trunk. The photograph must be a spring one
since the wood is full of wild garlic.

The Bear Inn, Rodborough, c. 1908. Before the extensive alterations which took place
between the wars, The Bear Inn looked much the same as it had for centuries. At this period
it hosted the Rodborough Bowling Club and, in the striped tin building on the left, the
headquarters of the Stroud Golf Club, which played on Rodborough Common. Golf had
ceased here by the 1930s and the club was disbanded. Note the tricycle by the main door.

Rodborough Common. Taken by Conway just outside The Bear Inn, the view seen in this photograph is almost unrecognizable today. The double-fronted house on the right has been demolished and all the others are now obscured by tall trees. For this reason, of course, the picture is significant.

Rodborough Manor. Built in the late eighteenth century by Onesiphorus Paul, a Woodchester clothier, this well-proportioned building was bought in 1855 by Lord John Russell, Member of Parliament for Stroud. The view shown here dates from around 1905.

x Scene of outbreak

Rodborough Manor Fire. The Manor was devastated by fire on 28 August 1906. According to contemporary newspaper reports, this broke out while the owner was playing billiards and spread quickly through the entire building. In this photograph Conway has helpfully marked where the fire originated.

Rodborough Manor Fire. In the aftermath of the disaster police and various servants are still in evidence and a ladder leans across the door.

Woodchester Valley.
From Amberley. 993.

The Woodchester Valley. This pleasant rural scene must date from shortly after the fire, since the roofless wreck of Rodborough Manor can be seen on the right.

Woodchester Priory. In the distance is the Dominican Priory, founded in the last century by the Leigh family of Woodchester Park. Today the church remains, but all the domestic buildings have been demolished. In the foreground, beyond the pony and trap, are the premises of Newman Hender and Company Limited.

Postscript: Dudbridge Station. If not on his bicycle, Conway would have used the local Midland Railway branch line to travel to Stroud or Gloucester. Here is the little station – now totally demolished – where passengers changed for Stroud. Note the re-used carriage on the left. This photograph is full of the atmosphere of Edwardian England – it could almost have been the set for E. Nesbit's *The Railway Children*. Such an evocative picture seems an appropriate conclusion to this study of Conway's work.